ARCTIC GROUND SQUIRREL

Table of Contents

Copyright © 2018

All rights reserved.

What Does the Arctic Ground Squirrel Look like?

The Arctic ground squirrel is a cute, furry animal that has fluffy beige and tan fur coat with special little white dots on its back. The Arctic ground squirrel has a short face with tiny little ears, cute little eyes with pretty white markings around them and a dark tail.

The Arctic ground squirrel changes its fur depending on whether its summer or winter. These fur changes help the Arctic ground squirrel blend in with the background better. As his winter coat begins to fall out for the summer, it is replaced by a cooler, finer coat. His summer coat has the colors red and yellow and in the winter these colors are replaced by silver instead.

The Arctic ground squirrel is about 39 cm long and has different weights depending on the time of year you weigh it. This is because the Arctic ground squirrel's weight changes with the season just like his coat. The reason why the Arctic ground squirrel has changing weight is that they like to eat a lot during autumn to increase its body fat to prepare for its hibernation during the freezing cold winter.

Where Does the Arctic Ground Squirrel Live?

The Arctic ground squirrels can be found in Northern Canada, Alaska and Siberia. These extremely cold areas without snow are the Arctic ground squirrels favourite place to live. The Arctic ground squirrels are quite special because it takes a strong animal to be able to survive the harsh weather conditions of the Arctic tundra.

What Does the Arctic Ground Squirrels Eat?

The Arctic ground squirrel enjoys eating grass, mushrooms, berries, roots, stalks and willows but its favourite are flowers and seeds. If you're lucky and the Arctic Ground Squirrel has been really greedy that day you might spot him storing food in his cheeks for a little snack later on or to store it inside his burrow!

The Arctic Ground Squirrel's Home

The Arctic ground squirrel's home is called a burrow.

To make a burrow, the Arctic ground squirrel digs a 3 feet deep underground and makes little secret rooms and tunnels with twists and turns like a little maze. The Arctic ground squirrel has to be extremely careful where it picks to build its burrow because if it rains and all the water goes inside then the poor Arctic ground squirrel would get wet and his home could collapse! Even more important is that the Arctic ground squirrel needs to make his home away from predators like foxes.

The Arctic ground squirrels store its food inside its burrow to have something to eat during spring as it waits for the plants to grow. The Arctic ground squirrel likes to live alone.

Arctic Ground Squirrel Babies

The Arctic ground squirrels look for a partner around May. A mommy Arctic ground squirrel is pregnant for 25 days and can have up 5 to 10 babies at one time. Baby Arctic ground squirrels are called pups. The babies are born with no hair and are blind. They live together with their mommy and drink her milk but only after 6 weeks old the tiny babies can start to eat grass and flowers. By the time they are 3 months old, they can live and survive by themselves. The little young squirrels need to eat a lot in order to gain much weight and grow up fast because they only have a couple of months before the weather turns really cold and they need to hibernate.

Adult squirrels are much better at finding food than young squirrels and for this reason most adults are able to build a burrow by August when they have already found plenty of food and are ready for that long sleep called hibernation. Young squirrels on the other hand take a long time to find all the food they need to be able to survive the harsh winter months and because they have never built a burrow this can take them a long time as well. This means that most young squirrels will not be able to settle inside their burrows until late September.

Arctic Ground Squirrel's Behaviour

Sometimes little squirrel pups can lose their mum and have nobody to look after them. Luckily for them quite often if a female squirrel finds them she will look after them and fetch them food as if she was their real mum. Male squirrels are a bit different though because they normally end up in fights with other male squirrels because they don't like other male squirrels playing on their area of land, this is called "being territorial."

What Eats the Arctic Ground Squirrel?

Big animals like eagles, foxes and even bears think the Arctic ground squirrels make a tasty meal.

To avoid being seen by their predators, the Arctic ground squirrels would make their bodies really flat and crawl across the ground in a move called the "tundra glide." When an Arctic ground squirrel gets attacked by a predator, it can warn other squirrels that danger is ahead by making certain noises. The Arctic ground squirrels can even make different noises depending on how they are being attacked; it makes a distinct sound if a bird is coming from the air and another sound if they are running from a grizzly bear.

The Arctic Ground Squirrel Hibernating in Winter

When the cold winter comes, the Arctic ground squirrels will settle inside their burrows. The Arctic ground squirrels can lower their body temperature to be colder than the temperature that water freezes at. When you go outside on an extremely cold day and see ice and snow the weather is under 0 to -1 degrees. This unique creature can cool himself to an amazing -3. This is the coldest body temperature that has ever been measured in a mammal. Scientists still don't know up to now how the Arctic ground squirrel can do it.

The Arctic ground squirrel as a mammal belongs to a group of animals who are warm blooded; this means they need to stay warm for them to live and be healthy. It is a great mystery how these little fellows can get themselves so cold and still be well afterwards. So as the Arctic ground squirrel settles down and goes to sleep, it cools its body down and its heartbeat starts to slow down too. Being too cold for a long time could make these poor little squirrels ill, so after a couple of weeks the Arctic ground squirrel will warm its body a little by shivering. It hibernates from the month of September up to April.

Once spring comes, the Arctic ground squirrels would shiver and shake back to their normal warm body temperature and slowly they start to wake up.

Now it is spring. The Arctic ground squirrel starts his journey all over again from going out of its burrow to finding a mate then having a litter of artic ground squirrel pups and taking care of it as they are born tiny and hairless to getting their fur and feeding them up until they can do it on their own.

The Arctic Ground Squirrel will then start searching for food before feeding himself up and getting big and fat before he builds a burrow and goes back to sleep for another seven months. The Arctic Ground Squirrel will do this circle of events over and over again. A male Arctic ground squirrel can live up to 6 years but the female Arctic ground squirrel can often live until 11 years old which is very old for such a small creature!

Disclaimer

Made in the USA
Monee, IL
04 February 2023

27134454R00017